Quicken Bible

The Complete Guide
to Budgeting, Expense
Tracking, and
Investments

Jeffrey G. H. Collen

TABLE OF CONTENTS

Quicken Bible

Introduction

Managing personal and business finances effectively is one of the most crucial skills in today's world. Whether you are an individual looking to take control of your household budget, a freelancer tracking income and expenses, or a small business owner managing multiple financial streams, having the right tool can make all the difference. **Quicken** has long been one of the most trusted and powerful financial management software solutions, offering a comprehensive suite of features to help users organize their financial lives with ease.

This guidebook is designed to take you through every aspect of Quicken, from basic setup to advanced features, ensuring that you can use the software to its full potential. With clear explanations, step-by-step instructions, real-world examples, and expert tips, you will gain the confidence and knowledge needed to manage your money efficiently.

Why Quicken? The Ultimate Financial Management Tool

In a world where financial uncertainty is a common concern, keeping track of every dollar is more important than ever. Quicken provides a **one-stop solution** for managing your income, expenses, investments, and budgets, making it easier to stay financially organized. Unlike generic budgeting apps, Quicken offers **powerful features** tailored for different financial needs, whether personal or business-related.

Comprehensive Money Management

Quicken is designed to help users gain a complete picture of their finances. By linking directly to your bank accounts, credit cards, loans, and investment portfolios, it allows you to track every transaction in real time. With **detailed reporting** and **customized budgeting tools**, you can make informed financial decisions with confidence.

Budgeting and Expense Tracking Made Simple

Many people struggle to stick to a budget because they don't have a clear overview of their spending habits. Quicken eliminates this problem by **automatically categorizing expenses**, helping you identify areas where you can cut costs or save more. With features such as **goal tracking** and **spending alerts**, Quicken ensures you stay on top of your finances effortlessly.

Investment and Retirement Planning

For those who invest in stocks, mutual funds, or retirement accounts, Quicken provides **advanced investment tracking tools** that allow you to monitor portfolio performance, calculate capital gains, and generate reports for tax planning. Whether you are planning for retirement or simply looking to optimize your investments, Quicken provides the insights you need to make informed decisions.

Business and Freelance Finance Management

Quicken isn't just for personal finance—it's also a powerful tool for small business owners and freelancers. With features such as **invoice tracking, tax deduction categorization, and business expense management**, it simplifies financial operations for entrepreneurs. It even integrates with tax software, ensuring accurate record-keeping and smooth tax preparation.

Automation and Time-Saving Features

One of Quicken's biggest advantages is automation. Users can **schedule bill payments, set up recurring transactions, and receive alerts for upcoming expenses**, reducing the need for manual data entry. With cloud syncing and mobile access, you can manage your finances **anytime, anywhere**, keeping financial stress to a minimum.

Security and Data Protection

Financial data security is a top priority, and Quicken ensures your information is **encrypted and securely stored**. Unlike web-based finance apps that store data online, Quicken allows for **local storage with backup options**, giving users more control over their financial records.

Who This Book Is For

This book is designed to cater to a wide range of users, from complete beginners to experienced Quicken users looking to master advanced features. Here's a breakdown of the key audiences who will benefit the most:

1. Individuals and Families

If you want to gain control over your household finances, Quicken provides all the tools you need to manage your income, expenses, and savings. This guide will show you how to set up a **realistic budget, track spending, and prepare for future financial goals**, such as buying a home, paying off debt, or saving for college tuition.

2. Freelancers and Self-Employed Professionals

Freelancers often juggle multiple income streams and expenses. This book provides **step-by-step guidance on using Quicken to track client payments, categorize business expenses for tax deductions, and generate profit and loss reports**, ensuring that managing freelance finances is no longer a hassle.

3. Small Business Owners

Quicken Home & Business is a powerful tool for entrepreneurs who need to **manage cash flow, track invoices, and separate personal and business expenses**. This guide will help business owners streamline their financial operations, ensuring they can focus on growth rather than paperwork.

4. Investors and Retirees

Whether you are a seasoned investor or someone planning for retirement, this book will teach you how to **track portfolio performance, monitor investment returns, and analyze tax implications using Quicken's advanced features**. Retirees can also learn how to **manage pension income, Social Security benefits, and healthcare expenses efficiently**.

5. Students and Young Adults

For students or young professionals just starting their financial journey, learning **how to budget, track expenses, and build good financial habits early on** is crucial. This book provides simple, practical strategies to help young users make the most of Quicken's tools.

6. Anyone Looking to Simplify Their Finances

If managing money has always seemed like a challenge, this guide will **help you break down financial management into simple, actionable steps**. Regardless of your background or experience level, you will learn how to use Quicken to its fullest potential and gain financial peace of mind.

How to Use This Guide for Maximum Benefit

This book is designed as a **step-by-step learning resource**, whether you are just getting started with Quicken or looking to unlock its most powerful features. To get the most out of this guide, consider the following approach:

1. Start with the Basics

If you are a beginner, it's important to start with the **foundational chapters on setup, expense tracking, and budgeting**. These sections will help you establish a strong understanding of

Quicken's core functionalities before moving on to more advanced topics.

2. Follow the Step-by-Step Walkthroughs

Each section includes **detailed, easy-to-follow instructions**, ensuring you can implement the concepts immediately. Many chapters contain **screenshots and real-world examples**, making it easier to visualize how Quicken works in practice.

3. Apply What You Learn

The best way to master Quicken is to **apply the knowledge to your own financial situation**. As you read through each chapter, try out the features on your own Quicken software. Whether it's setting up an account, categorizing expenses, or generating reports, hands-on practice will help reinforce your learning.

4. Use the Troubleshooting Guides and Expert Tips

Throughout the book, you will find **common troubleshooting solutions and expert insights** to help you avoid mistakes and make the most of Quicken's capabilities. These tips will save you time and frustration, ensuring a smoother experience with the software.

5. Explore Advanced Features as You Progress

Once you are comfortable with the basics, dive into the **more advanced sections, such as investment tracking, tax planning, and automation**. These features will help you optimize Quicken for long-term financial success.

6. Refer to Companion Resources

At the end of this book, you will **recommended tools** to further enhance your financial management skills. These additional resources will complement what you learn in the book, making financial planning even easier.

By following this guide, you will be well-equipped to **use Quicken efficiently, gain financial clarity, and achieve long-term financial success**. Whether you are looking to manage a personal budget, grow a business, or plan for retirement, this book will serve as your **ultimate Quicken companion**.

Getting Started with Quicken

Quicken is one of the most powerful financial management tools available today, offering a suite of features that help individuals, families, and businesses track their finances with ease. However, to fully leverage its capabilities, it is important to start with a **solid foundation**. This chapter will walk you through the process of choosing the right version of Quicken, installing it correctly, setting up your account, linking bank accounts, and navigating the interface so you can begin managing your finances efficiently.

Choosing the Right Version of Quicken

Before you begin using Quicken, it's crucial to select the version that best fits your financial needs. Quicken offers several editions, each catering to different levels of personal and business finance management. Understanding the differences between these versions will ensure you get the most value from the software.

1. Quicken Starter

Best for: Individuals who need basic budgeting and expense tracking.

- Allows users to **track income and expenses** by manually entering transactions.
- Provides basic **budgeting tools** to help monitor spending.
- **Limited bank connectivity**—some financial institutions may not support automatic transaction downloads.
- No investment tracking or advanced business features.

Ideal for users who are just starting with financial management and want a simple, no-frills budgeting tool.

2. Quicken Deluxe

Best for: Individuals and families who want advanced budgeting and financial planning.

- Includes all the features of **Starter**, plus:
    - **Automatic bank transaction downloads**, reducing manual entry.
    - **Debt tracking tools**, helping users pay off loans more effectively.
    - **Savings goal setting** for future financial planning.
    - Customizable **budgeting and financial reports**.

A great choice for those who need more control over their finances but don't require investment tracking.

3. Quicken Premier

Best for: Investors and individuals with more complex financial needs.

- Includes all **Deluxe** features, plus:
  - ○ **Investment tracking**, including stocks, bonds, mutual funds, and retirement accounts.
  - ○ **Capital gains calculations** and **performance analysis**.
  - ○ **Tax planning tools**, helping users track deductions and prepare tax reports.

Perfect for users with investment portfolios who want in-depth financial insights.

4. Quicken Home & Business

Best for: Small business owners, freelancers, and landlords.

- Includes all **Premier** features, plus:
  - ○ **Business income and expense tracking**.

○ **Invoice and payment
   management** for freelancers and
   small business owners.
○ **Rental property management**
   features, including tenant tracking.

This version is ideal for entrepreneurs who want
to **separate personal and business finances**
while taking advantage of Quicken's full suite of
tools.

Which Version Should You Choose?

- **If you only need budgeting and expense
  tracking** → Starter or Deluxe.
- **If you have investments and want
  financial insights** → Premier.
- **If you own a business or rental property**
  → Home & Business.

System Requirements and Installation Guide

Before installing Quicken, make sure your system meets the software's requirements to ensure smooth performance.

System Requirements

Windows

- **Operating System:** Windows 10 or later
- **Processor:** 1GHz or higher
- **RAM:** 2GB (4GB or more recommended)
- **Hard Disk Space:** At least 450MB
- **Internet Connection:** Required for downloads, updates, and online banking

Mac

- **Operating System:** macOS 11 (Big Sur) or later
- **Processor:** Intel-based or Apple Silicon Mac
- **RAM:** 4GB or more
- **Hard Disk Space:** At least 450MB
- **Internet Connection:** Required for online features

Installation Guide

For Windows Users:

1. **Purchase and Download Quicken**

   - Buy Quicken from the **official website** or a reputable retailer.
   - Download the installer from your Quicken account.

2. **Run the Installer**

   - Locate the **Quicken.exe** file in your Downloads folder.
   - Double-click the file to launch the installation process.

3. **Follow Setup Instructions**

   - Accept the license agreement.
   - Choose an installation location (default is recommended).
   - Click **Install** and wait for the process to complete.

4. **Sign In or Create a Quicken Account**

- ○ Launch Quicken and sign in using your **Quicken ID**.
- ○ If you don't have an account, create one by following the on-screen prompts.

For Mac Users:

1. Download the **Quicken.dmg** file from the official website.
2. Open the **dmg file** and drag the Quicken icon into the **Applications folder**.
3. Launch Quicken from **Applications** and sign in with your Quicken ID.

Setting Up Your Quicken Account and Linking Bank Accounts

Once Quicken is installed, the next step is to set up your account and link it to your financial institutions.

1. Creating a New Quicken File

- Open Quicken and click **File > New Quicken File**.
- Choose a **name and location** for your file.
- Select **Create** to start a fresh financial database.

2. Adding Bank Accounts

Quicken allows you to connect to thousands of financial institutions for automatic transaction downloads.

Steps to Link a Bank Account:

1. Click **Accounts > Add Account**.
2. Select your account type (Checking, Savings, Credit Card, Investment, etc.).
3. Search for your bank and click **Connect**.
4. Enter your online banking credentials (username and password).
5. Quicken will **fetch** your transactions automatically.

If your bank does not support direct downloads, you can manually import transactions by downloading **QFX files** from your bank's website.

Navigating the Quicken Interface: A Tour of the Dashboard

Understanding Quicken's interface will help you navigate its features quickly and efficiently.

1. Home Dashboard

The **Home** screen provides a financial overview, including:

- **Account balances**
- **Spending trends**
- **Upcoming bills and reminders**

You can customize the dashboard to display only the widgets you need.

2. Accounts Bar

Located on the left side, the **Accounts Bar** lists all connected financial accounts. Clicking on an account shows **detailed transactions** and **balances**.

3. Spending Tab

The **Spending** section categorizes expenses, allowing you to see **where your money is going**.

4. Bills & Income Tab

This section helps track **upcoming bills, income, and recurring payments**.

5. Budgeting Section

Users can create and manage budgets, set financial goals, and **track progress over time**.

6. Investments Tab

If you have **Premier or Home & Business**, the Investments tab displays **portfolio performance, stock trends, and asset allocation**.

7. Reports & Graphs

Quicken offers powerful **customizable reports**, including:

- Spending reports
- Income vs. expenses
- Net worth analysis

8. Syncing with Mobile and Cloud

Quicken allows users to sync data to **mobile devices**, ensuring access to financial information on the go.

Mastering Expense Tracking in Quicken

Effective financial management starts with **accurate expense tracking**. Without a clear understanding of where your money goes, budgeting, saving, and investing can become difficult. Quicken provides powerful tools to **track every dollar**, categorize expenses, and generate detailed reports that help you stay on top of your finances. This chapter covers the essential skills needed to master expense tracking, from adding and categorizing transactions to reconciling bank data and generating cash flow reports.

Adding, Editing, and Categorizing Transactions

1. Manually Adding Transactions

While Quicken can automatically import bank transactions, there may be times when you need to enter transactions manually, such as **cash purchases, checks, or personal loans**.

Steps to Add a Transaction Manually:

1. **Select the account** where the transaction occurred (e.g., checking, credit card).
2. Click **"Add Transaction"** or **"New"** (depending on your Quicken version).
3. Fill in the required details:
   - **Date:** The date of the transaction.
   - **Payee:** The recipient (e.g., store, utility company, individual).
   - **Category:** Choose an appropriate category (e.g., groceries, rent, entertainment).

- ○ **Amount:** Enter the amount spent or received.
- ○ **Payment Method:** Cash, check, or card.
- ○ **Memo/Notes:** Add extra details if needed.
4. Click **Save** to store the transaction.

This method ensures **accurate record-keeping**, especially for transactions that are not automatically synced.

2. Editing Transactions

If you make an error in a transaction or need to update information, you can easily edit existing records.

Steps to Edit a Transaction:

1. Navigate to the **account register** where the transaction is recorded.
2. Locate the transaction and **double-click** it.
3. Modify the necessary fields (e.g., amount, payee, category).
4. Click **Save** to update the changes.

3. Categorizing Transactions

Proper categorization is crucial for **accurate budgeting and financial analysis.** Quicken offers a robust system of predefined categories and allows users to create custom categories for more precise tracking.

Choosing Categories

When entering a transaction, select an appropriate category such as:

- **Groceries** (for food purchases)
- **Utilities** (for electricity, water, and internet bills)
- **Entertainment** (for movies, dining out, and subscriptions)
- **Income: Salary** (for regular paycheck deposits)
- **Investment: Dividends** (for dividend earnings)

4. Creating Custom Categories

If the default categories do not meet your needs, you can create new ones.

Steps to Create a Custom Category:

1. Go to **Tools > Category List**.
2. Click **New Category**.
3. Enter a **Category Name** and select a **Parent Category** (if applicable).
4. Choose whether it is an **Income or Expense** category.
5. Click **OK** to save.

By customizing categories, you gain **better insights into your spending habits** and improve budgeting accuracy.

Using Tags and Notes for Better Organization

1. What Are Tags in Quicken?

Tags allow you to add extra layers of classification to transactions. Unlike categories, tags are **flexible and can be applied across different categories**.

For example, you might have expenses in different categories related to a **family vacation** (e.g., flights under "Travel" and dining under "Restaurants"). You can tag all these expenses with **"Vacation 2024"** to track them as a group.

How to Use Tags:

1. When entering a transaction, find the **Tag field**.
2. Type a **descriptive tag** (e.g., "Wedding Expenses" or "Tax Deductible").
3. Click **Save**.
4. Later, use Quicken's **Tag Reports** to filter transactions by tag.

2. Adding Notes and Memos

Quicken allows users to add notes to transactions for better context.

- **Example 1:** For a **charitable donation,** you can add a memo like "Tax deductible donation for 2024."
- **Example 2:** For a **shared expense**, you can add "Dinner with John, he owes $50."

To add notes:

1. Open a transaction.
2. Locate the **Memo/Notes field**.
3. Enter a description.
4. Click **Save**.

Using notes and tags ensures you **never forget the purpose of a transaction**, making budgeting and financial analysis much easier.

Importing and Reconciling Bank Transactions

Quicken allows users to **import transactions directly from their bank accounts**, reducing manual data entry and errors. However, it is essential to **reconcile transactions** to ensure all records are accurate.

1. Importing Bank Transactions

Many banks support direct **download and sync** with Quicken.

Steps to Import Transactions Automatically:

1. Click **Accounts > Update Accounts**.
2. Enter your **bank credentials** if prompted.
3. Quicken will download **recent transactions**.
4. Review each transaction and ensure categories are correct.

2. Manually Importing Bank Transactions (QFX Files)

If your bank does not support automatic syncing, you can manually import transactions.

Steps to Manually Import Transactions:

1. Log in to your **bank's website**.

2. Download your transaction history in
   QFX format.
3. Open Quicken and go to **File > Import >
   Bank Transactions**.
4. Select the downloaded **QFX file** and click
   Import.
5. Review and categorize transactions.

3. Reconciling Transactions

Reconciliation ensures that **Quicken matches
your bank statement**, preventing discrepancies.

Steps to Reconcile Your Account:

1. Click on the **account** you want to
   reconcile.
2. Select **Tools > Reconcile**.
3. Enter the **ending balance and statement
   date** from your bank statement.
4. Match transactions in Quicken with those
   on the statement.
5. If there are **missing or incorrect
   transactions**, edit them accordingly.
6. Click **Finish** when everything matches.

Regular reconciliation **prevents errors**, identifies fraudulent transactions, and ensures accurate financial records.

Understanding Cash Flow Reports

A **cash flow report** helps you track how money moves in and out of your accounts, giving a clear picture of **income vs. expenses** over time.

1. Generating a Cash Flow Report in Quicken

1. Click **Reports > Spending > Cash Flow Report**.
2. Select a **time period** (monthly, quarterly, yearly).
3. Customize filters such as **accounts, categories, and tags**.
4. Click **Generate Report**.

2. Analyzing the Cash Flow Report

A typical cash flow report includes:

- **Income Sources:** Salary, dividends, rental income, etc.
- **Fixed Expenses:** Mortgage, rent, insurance premiums.
- **Variable Expenses:** Groceries, dining, entertainment.
- **Net Cash Flow:** The difference between income and expenses.

3. Using Cash Flow Reports for Financial Planning

- If **expenses exceed income**, identify areas to **cut back on spending**.
- If you have a **positive cash flow**, allocate surplus funds to **savings or investments**.
- Track trends over time to **predict future financial stability**.

Budgeting Like a Pro in Quicken

A well-planned budget is the foundation of financial success. Whether you're managing personal expenses, a household budget, or business finances, Quicken provides powerful tools to help you stay on track. Budgeting in Quicken is more than just tracking expenses—it's about setting financial goals, automating alerts, and analyzing trends to make informed decisions. This chapter will take you through everything you need to know about creating, managing, and optimizing your budget in Quicken.

Creating a Realistic Budget in Quicken

1. Why Budgeting Matters

A budget helps you:

- **Understand where your money goes**
- **Identify unnecessary expenses**
- **Save for short-term and long-term goals**
- **Plan for major life events (buying a home, starting a business, retirement, etc.)**
- **Avoid financial stress by preparing for emergencies**

2. Steps to Create a Budget in Quicken

Step 1: Open the Budget Tool

1. Go to **Tools > Budget** in Quicken.
2. Click **Create a New Budget** or **Start a Budget Plan** if it's your first time.

Step 2: Choose Your Budget Type

Quicken offers different types of budgets depending on your needs:

- **Monthly Budget:** Ideal for tracking day-to-day expenses.
- **Annual Budget:** Useful for long-term financial planning.
- **Business Budget:** Designed for business owners and self-employed individuals.

Step 3: Select Accounts to Include

Decide which accounts should be part of your budget. You can include:

- Checking and savings accounts
- Credit cards
- Investment accounts (optional)

Step 4: Set Income and Expense Categories

- Quicken will suggest **income and expense categories** based on your past transactions.
- You can adjust or add new categories to fit your needs.

For example:

- **Income Categories:** Salary, freelance work, rental income, dividends.
- **Expense Categories:** Mortgage, groceries, utilities, entertainment, savings contributions.

Step 5: Set Budget Amounts

- Enter the expected monthly or yearly amount for each category.
- Use past spending trends in Quicken's reports to make realistic estimates.

Step 6: Adjust and Finalize

- Review the **Budget Summary** to see if your income covers expenses.
- Adjust any unrealistic budget limits.
- Click **Save & Close** to finalize your budget.

Setting Up and Tracking Budget Goals

A budget isn't just about limiting spending—it's also about setting **financial goals**. Quicken makes it easy to create and monitor goals such as **saving for a vacation, paying off debt, or investing for retirement**.

1. How to Create a Budget Goal

1. Go to **Tools > Savings Goals**.
2. Click **Create a New Goal**.
3. Select the type of goal:
    - Emergency Fund
    - Vacation
    - Home Down Payment
    - Debt Repayment
    - Retirement Savings
4. Enter the target amount and desired completion date.
5. Choose the **funding source** (bank account, savings, investment account).
6. Click **Save & Track**.

2. Tracking Progress on Budget Goals

- Quicken automatically updates your progress as you make contributions.
- You can view your progress in **Reports > Goals Progress Report**.
- Adjust contributions if needed based on changes in income and expenses.

3. Example Budget Goals

- **Saving for a $5,000 vacation in 12 months** → Requires saving **$416 per month**.
- **Paying off a $10,000 credit card debt in 24 months** → Requires monthly payments of **$416 plus interest**.

By setting and tracking goals, you can stay motivated and on course to **financial success**.

Automating Budget Alerts and Notifications

To stay on top of your budget, Quicken offers **automation features** that notify you of important budget updates.

1. Why Automate Budget Alerts?

Automating budget alerts helps you:

- Stay within your spending limits.
- Avoid overdrafts and unnecessary fees.
- Adjust your budget when unexpected expenses arise.

2. How to Set Up Budget Alerts in Quicken

1. Go to **Edit > Preferences > Alerts & Messages**.
2. Choose **Budget Alerts** from the menu.
3. Enable alerts for:
   - **Overspending in a category** (e.g., spending more than $200 on dining).
   - **Reaching your monthly budget limit**.
   - **Low account balances**.
   - **Upcoming bills and due dates**.
4. Select how you want to receive alerts:
   - **On-screen pop-ups**
   - **Email notifications**

- ○ Mobile alerts (if using Quicken mobile app)

3. Example Budget Alerts

- "You've spent 90% of your grocery budget for the month."
- "Your checking account balance is below $500."
- "Your credit card bill is due in 3 days."

These alerts **help you stay proactive** and make adjustments before a financial issue arises.

Analyzing Budget Trends Over Time

Tracking budget trends over months and years can help you **identify spending patterns, plan for future expenses, and make informed financial decisions**.

1. How to Generate Budget Reports in Quicken

1. Go to **Reports > Spending > Budget vs. Actual Report**.
2. Select a time frame (monthly, quarterly, yearly).
3. Choose the accounts and categories you want to analyze.
4. Click **Generate Report**.

2. Understanding Budget Trend Reports

A **budget trend report** compares your projected budget with actual spending, showing:

- **Areas where you overspend** (e.g., dining out, entertainment).
- **Areas where you underspend** (e.g., savings, investments).
- **Fluctuations in income and expenses** over time.

3. Using Trends to Improve Your Budget

- **If you consistently exceed your dining budget**, consider cooking more at home.

- **If you underspend in one category**, you may be able to redirect funds to savings or investments.
- **If income varies significantly month-to-month**, plan ahead for lower-income months by setting aside surplus income.

4. Example Budget Trend Insights

- **Seasonal fluctuations:** Higher utility bills in winter, higher travel expenses in summer.
- **Rising costs:** Noticing a gradual increase in grocery or fuel expenses.
- **Spending habits:** Identifying unnecessary subscriptions or impulse purchases.

By regularly reviewing budget trends, you can make **data-driven adjustments** to your financial plan.

Managing Bills and Payments Efficiently in Quicken

Efficient bill management is key to maintaining financial stability and avoiding unnecessary stress. Late payments, missed bills, and unorganized financial records can have a significant impact on your credit score, finances, and mental well-being. Fortunately, Quicken offers a suite of tools to streamline the management of your bills and payments, making it easier to stay on top of due dates, automate payments, and track recurring transactions. This chapter will guide you through managing your bills and payments efficiently using Quicken's powerful features.

Setting Up and Automating Bill Payments

1. Why Automate Bill Payments?

Automating your bill payments offers several key advantages:

- **Avoid Late Fees**: Quicken helps you set up automatic payments for your recurring bills, ensuring that payments are made on time, every time.
- **Save Time**: No more manual tracking of due dates and logging into multiple accounts to pay bills.
- **Improve Credit Score**: Timely payments directly affect your credit score, which is crucial for securing loans, mortgages, and other financial opportunities.

- **Reduce Mental Load**: Automating your payments means fewer worries about missing deadlines or managing complex due dates.

2. How to Set Up Bill Payment Automation in Quicken

To set up automated bill payments in Quicken:

1. **Link Your Accounts**:

   - Ensure your bank and credit card accounts are linked to Quicken under **Accounts > Add Account**.
   - Quicken will sync your transactions, including recurring payments, directly from your bank.

2. **Add Billers and Set Payment Preferences**:

   - Navigate to **Bills & Income > Bill Manager > Add Bill**.

- ○ Choose a **Biller** from the list or
  manually add the name of your
  service provider.
- ○ Enter the payment amount, due
  date, and frequency (monthly,
  quarterly, etc.).
- ○ Select your payment method (e.g.,
  linked bank account, credit card, or
  PayPal).

3. **Enable Automatic Payments**:

- ○ Choose **Auto Pay** to automatically
  pay bills on their due dates.
- ○ Review the bill's details before
  confirming to ensure the amount
  and payment method are correct.

4. **Set Up Notifications and Alerts**:

- ○ Quicken allows you to receive
  notifications when a payment is
  approaching, so you can confirm
  that everything is set.

○ To enable these, go to **Edit > Preferences > Alerts & Messages** and turn on bill payment reminders.

3. Managing Scheduled Payments

Once automated payments are set up, Quicken will automatically deduct the payment from your chosen account and send you a confirmation. You can view upcoming payments and scheduled transactions by navigating to **Bills & Income > Bill Manager > Scheduled Bills**. From here, you can:

- **Edit Payment Information**: Change the payment amount, frequency, or due date.
- **Pause or Skip Payments**: Temporarily halt automated payments, if needed.
- **Review History**: Check past payments for accuracy and completeness.

By automating your payments, you can simplify your financial life and ensure that bills are always paid on time.

Tracking Due Dates and Avoiding Late Fees

1. The Importance of Tracking Due Dates

Missing a bill's due date can lead to costly late fees, disrupted services, and a negative impact on your credit score. Tracking due dates effectively is essential to avoid these problems, and Quicken provides an easy way to monitor all of your upcoming bills.

2. How to Track Due Dates in Quicken

1. **Set Up Bill Reminders**:

   - In Quicken, go to **Bills & Income > Bill Manager > Add Reminder**.
   - Input the **due date** and the **frequency** (e.g., monthly, quarterly, annually).
   - Add the payment **amount** and your preferred **payment method**.
   - Set a reminder notification for a few days before the bill is due, so

you have time to review the
payment.

2. **Bill Payment Calendar**:

   ○ Quicken's **Bill Payment Calendar**
   is a convenient way to visually
   track upcoming due dates.
   ○ Go to **Bills & Income > Bill
   Manager > Calendar View**.
   ○ You can filter bills by account,
   status (paid or unpaid), and due
   date.
   ○ The calendar view will give you a
   clear, at-a-glance overview of all
   your bills for the month, helping
   you avoid surprises.

3. **Track and Pay on Time**:

   ○ When the payment due date is
   approaching, Quicken will
   automatically send a reminder.
   ○ If you have **auto-pay enabled**,
   Quicken will take care of the
   payment for you.

○ If not, you can manually approve the payment with just a few clicks.

By staying on top of your bill due dates with Quicken's reminder and calendar features, you can eliminate the risk of late fees and ensure your bills are always paid on time.

Managing Recurring Transactions

1. The Power of Recurring Transactions in Quicken

Recurring transactions are any payments or income that occur regularly, such as rent, mortgage payments, utility bills, and subscriptions. Managing these transactions efficiently ensures that you can plan for them without forgetting or overestimating your available balance.

2. How to Set Up Recurring Transactions in Quicken

To set up a recurring transaction in Quicken, follow these steps:

1. **Navigate to Transactions**:

   - Go to **Tools > Recurring Transactions** and select **Create New Transaction**.
2. **Enter the Transaction Details**:

   - Choose the **category, payee**, and **amount** for the recurring transaction.
   - Specify whether the transaction is an **income** or an **expense**.
   - Set the **frequency** (e.g., weekly, monthly, quarterly).
   - Enter the **start and end date** for the recurring transaction.
3. **Customize the Recurrence**:

   - Quicken gives you full control over how often a transaction repeats. You can choose to repeat it:

- **Daily**: For daily payments like subscriptions.
- **Weekly/Monthly**: For rent, utilities, or credit card payments.
- **Annually**: For annual payments such as insurance or property taxes.

4. **Save and Review Recurring Transactions**:

   - Once you've set up the recurring transaction, Quicken will automatically record it each time it's due.
   - You can view and manage all your recurring transactions in **Tools > Recurring Transactions**.

By utilizing Quicken's recurring transaction feature, you can save time and ensure that all regular payments are properly accounted for. This feature reduces the chances of missing or mismanaging recurring expenses.

Using Quicken's Bill Manager for Seamless Payments

1. What is Bill Manager?

Quicken's **Bill Manager** is a comprehensive tool designed to streamline the process of managing and paying bills. It combines several key features—bill reminders, payment automation, and transaction history—into one easy-to-use interface.

2. How to Use Bill Manager in Quicken

1. **Accessing Bill Manager:**

   - Navigate to **Bills & Income > Bill Manager**.
   - Bill Manager will automatically pull up a list of your recurring bills and payments.

2. **Adding New Bills:**

- ○ Click **Add Bill** to manually input a new bill that isn't already tracked in Quicken.
- ○ Enter details like **bill type** (e.g., utilities, mortgage), **due date**, and **payment amount**.
- ○ Quicken will remember this information for future payments.

3. **Review and Pay Bills**:

- ○ Quicken will display upcoming bills and allow you to make payments directly from the app.
- ○ Select the bill you want to pay, confirm the payment amount, and choose your payment method (linked account or credit card).
- ○ Quicken will automatically send the payment to the appropriate biller.

4. **Tracking Payment Status**:

- ○ Bill Manager also lets you track **paid bills, pending payments**, and **overdue bills**.

○ Review your payment history and
view detailed **transaction reports**
for easy reference.

3. Benefits of Using Bill Manager

- **Consolidate All Bills in One Place**:
Track all your recurring bills from various
sources in a single dashboard.
- **Seamless Payments**: Make payments
directly through Quicken without the need
for external tools or apps.
- **Payment History**: Quickly access past
payments and track your payment habits.
- **Avoid Late Fees**: Automated payment
scheduling ensures that you never miss a
due date again.

Tracking and Growing Your Investments with Quicken

Managing your investments effectively is a crucial part of building long-term wealth and securing financial freedom. Whether you are an experienced investor or just starting out, Quicken provides powerful tools that allow you to track and grow your investment portfolio, ensuring that your money works for you. This chapter will guide you through setting up your investment accounts in Quicken, monitoring different asset classes, analyzing portfolio performance, and managing tax implications such as dividends, capital gains, and tax-loss harvesting.

Setting Up Investment Accounts in Quicken

1. Why Track Investments in Quicken?

Tracking your investments accurately is essential for several reasons:

- **Consolidated Overview**: With Quicken, you can view all of your investments in one place, including stocks, bonds, mutual funds, and retirement accounts.
- **Performance Monitoring**: By regularly tracking your investments, you can monitor their performance and make informed decisions based on real-time data.
- **Tax Efficiency**: Quicken's reporting features help you stay on top of tax

liabilities, making tax season less stressful.

2. How to Set Up an Investment Account in Quicken

To begin tracking your investments in Quicken, follow these steps:

1. **Create an Investment Account**:

    ○ Navigate to **Accounts > Add Account**.
    ○ Select **Investment Account** from the list of available account types.
    ○ Choose whether you are setting up an account for personal use or for retirement (IRA, 401(k), etc.).
    ○ Input the **account details**, such as account name, institution, and account number (if applicable).

2. **Link Your Investment Accounts**:

    ○ Quicken can automatically sync with most financial institutions, including brokerages and retirement account providers.

- ○ After selecting your investment provider, enter your login credentials to link your account.
- ○ If your institution is not supported, you can manually add your investments by entering them as individual transactions.

3. **Enter Investments into the Account**:

- ○ Once your account is set up, you can start entering your investments.
- ○ For **stocks and mutual funds**, input the purchase date, price, and number of shares.
- ○ For **bonds**, enter the bond's type, interest rate, and maturity date.
- ○ For **retirement accounts**, input the details of your contributions, distributions, and any employer match.

By setting up investment accounts correctly, you'll be able to see your entire portfolio's performance in one place and monitor your progress toward your financial goals.

Monitoring Stocks, Mutual Funds, and Retirement Accounts

1. Tracking Different Types of Investments

Quicken makes it easy to track a wide variety of investments, from individual stocks to diversified mutual funds and retirement accounts. Here's how to monitor each of them:

Stocks

- **Automatic Updates**: Quicken automatically retrieves the current market value of individual stocks and displays it in your portfolio.
- **Buy/Sell Transactions**: Track the purchase and sale of stocks by entering the transaction details (date, quantity,

price). Quicken will calculate the cost basis and help you track gains or losses.

- **Real-Time Prices**: Quicken syncs with market data providers to give you real-time stock prices, so you can stay on top of the market.

Mutual Funds

- **Net Asset Value (NAV)**: Quicken retrieves the NAV for mutual funds from your financial institution, showing you the current value per share.
- **Capital Gains and Distributions**: Quicken tracks your mutual fund distributions, including capital gains and dividend payments, ensuring that they are recorded accurately for tax purposes.
- **Fund Performance**: You can view your fund's performance over time, including annual returns and year-to-date performance.

Retirement Accounts

- **IRA, 401(k), and Other Accounts**: Quicken allows you to track tax-advantaged retirement accounts, including IRAs and 401(k)s, along with traditional brokerage accounts.
- **Contribution Tracking**: Track your contributions to retirement accounts, including employer contributions (if applicable), and monitor your progress toward retirement goals.
- **Required Minimum Distributions (RMDs)**: Quicken helps you track RMDs for retirement accounts to avoid penalties.

2. Syncing Multiple Accounts

To maintain an updated and accurate investment portfolio, Quicken allows you to sync multiple investment accounts from different institutions.

- Go to **Tools > Online Services** and connect your various accounts.
- You'll be able to see a consolidated view of your portfolio, making it easier to

assess your asset allocation and
diversification.

Analyzing Portfolio Performance with Reports and Graphs

1. Importance of Portfolio Analysis

Analyzing your investment portfolio is essential
for making informed decisions about asset
allocation, risk management, and financial goals.
Quicken offers a range of tools to help you
assess the performance of your investments.

2. Portfolio Performance Reports

Quicken generates detailed reports to help you
track your investment performance over time.
Some key reports to use include:

Performance Report

- This report shows the overall return of your investment portfolio, including capital gains, dividends, and interest.
- It includes both realized and unrealized gains, giving you a complete picture of your portfolio's performance.

Asset Allocation Report

- This report breaks down your portfolio into various asset classes (stocks, bonds, cash, real estate, etc.).
- It helps you understand how well-diversified your portfolio is and whether it aligns with your financial goals and risk tolerance.

Investment Summary Report

- Provides a quick summary of each of your individual investments, including total value, current holdings, and performance metrics.

- Helps you evaluate how each asset contributes to your overall portfolio performance.

3. Graphs for Visual Insights

Quicken's built-in graphs offer visual insights into your portfolio's performance:

- **Portfolio Value Graph**: Shows the change in value of your entire portfolio over time.
- **Performance vs. Benchmark Graph**: Compares your portfolio's performance against a relevant benchmark index (e.g., S&P 500).
- **Asset Allocation Pie Chart**: Provides a visual representation of how your portfolio is allocated across different asset classes.

Using these reports and graphs, you can quickly assess how your investments are performing and make data-driven decisions to optimize your portfolio.

Managing Dividends, Capital Gains, and Tax-Loss Harvesting

1. Tracking Dividends and Capital Gains

Dividends and capital gains are critical components of investment returns, and they also have tax implications. Quicken helps you manage both by automatically tracking them and categorizing them for tax purposes.

Dividends

- Quicken automatically records dividend payments from your investments and categorizes them as income.
- You can see the total dividends earned from each investment and track their growth over time.
- For tax purposes, dividends are classified into **qualified** and **non-qualified** dividends, which are taxed differently.

Capital Gains

- Quicken calculates your **capital gains** based on your investment sales, tracking both **long-term** and **short-term** gains.
- The program calculates your **cost basis**, ensuring accurate tax reporting when you sell investments.
- For each sale, Quicken tracks your **purchase price** and **sale price**, helping you calculate your gain or loss.

2. Tax-Loss Harvesting

Tax-loss harvesting is a strategy used to reduce taxes by selling investments that have declined in value, thus offsetting taxable gains. Quicken makes it easy to identify opportunities for tax-loss harvesting.

How Quicken Helps with Tax-Loss Harvesting

- **Tax Reports**: Quicken provides **capital gains** and **tax reports** that show which investments have been sold at a loss.

- **Tax-Loss Harvesting Alerts**: You can set up alerts in Quicken to notify you when there are opportunities for tax-loss harvesting.
- **Offsetting Gains**: By strategically selling investments that have declined in value, you can use those losses to offset gains in other parts of your portfolio, reducing your overall tax liability.

3. Managing Investment Income and Taxes

- **Tax Reports**: Quicken generates reports that categorize your investment income (dividends, interest, and capital gains) and assigns them to the appropriate tax categories.
- **Tax Deduction Tracking**: Quicken tracks investment-related tax deductions, such as those for investment interest or tax-loss harvesting, so you can maximize your tax efficiency.

Using Quicken for Small Business and Freelancers

Managing finances for a small business or freelance career can be challenging, particularly when trying to balance income, expenses, tax deductions, and cash flow. Quicken offers an array of tools to help small business owners and freelancers manage their finances with ease, providing a comprehensive view of their financial health. Whether you're a solo entrepreneur or running a small team, Quicken can help streamline your accounting tasks, allowing you to focus on growth and productivity. This chapter will walk you through how to set up business accounts, track invoices, manage business expenses, and generate financial reports to ensure that your business remains financially sound.

Setting Up Business Accounts and Categories

1. Why Business Accounts in Quicken?

Tracking your business finances separately from your personal finances is essential for accurate reporting, easier tax preparation, and clearer financial management. Quicken makes it simple to set up business accounts, categorize your business transactions, and ensure that you stay organized year-round.

2. How to Set Up a Business Account in Quicken

1. **Create a New Business Account**:

   - Navigate to **Accounts > Add Account** in Quicken.

- ○ Select **Business Account** from the options.
- ○ Enter the details of your business account, such as the name of the business, account type (checking, savings, credit card), and the financial institution associated with the account.
- ○ You can choose to link this account with your financial institution for automatic downloads of transactions, or you can manually enter transactions if you prefer.

2. **Business Account Types**:

- ○ **Checking Account**: For your day-to-day business transactions. It allows you to pay bills, make deposits, and track income and expenses.
- ○ **Credit Card Account**: If you use a credit card for business expenses, set this account up separately so

you can easily track payments and purchases related to your business.

- ○ **Savings Account**: For separating savings specifically set aside for taxes, future business expenses, or investments.
- ○ **Loan Account**: For tracking any loans or lines of credit your business has taken out.

3. Categorizing Business Transactions

1. **Business Categories**:
   To keep your business finances organized, you'll need to set up business-specific categories for both income and expenses. Quicken allows you to create custom categories such as:

   - ○ **Income**: Sales revenue, service fees, product sales.
   - ○ **Expenses**: Marketing, office supplies, client meetings, subscriptions, salaries (if applicable).

○ **Tax Deductions**: Quicken can help you categorize expenses that are tax-deductible, such as business mileage, office equipment, or business-related meals and entertainment.

2. **Using Subcategories**: Subcategories allow you to break down larger categories into more specific groups, such as breaking down **marketing** expenses into **online ads** or **print ads**, making it easier to track and analyze where your money is going.

3. **Creating Custom Tags and Notes**: Quicken also allows you to use **tags** and **notes** for further categorization. This feature is particularly useful if you need to track specific projects, clients, or business activities that require detailed tracking beyond standard categories.

Tracking Invoices and Payments from Clients

1. Importance of Invoicing and Payment Tracking

For any small business or freelancer, consistent cash flow is key to maintaining operations. Quicken offers tools to help you track invoices, monitor payments, and follow up with clients. This ensures that your income remains stable and that you stay on top of what is owed to you.

2. Creating and Managing Invoices

1. **How to Create an Invoice**:

   - In Quicken, you can create professional-looking invoices for your clients, ensuring that they include all relevant details, such as:
     - Client name and contact information.
     - Invoice date and due date.
     - Services or products provided and their associated costs.

- Total amount due, including taxes or additional charges (if applicable).
- You can customize invoices with your business logo and branding to give them a professional touch.
- Quicken allows you to send invoices directly to clients via email or print them for physical delivery.

2. **Tracking Invoice Status**:

- Quicken automatically tracks the status of invoices, allowing you to see which ones have been paid, which are outstanding, and which are overdue.
- You can set **due dates** for each invoice and enable **reminders** in Quicken to help you stay on top of late payments.
- Quicken also allows you to create **payment terms** for each client, whether you want payment due

immediately, within 30 days, or on a different schedule.

3. Payment Methods and Processing

1. Recording Payments:

- When you receive payment from clients, whether by check, credit card, or bank transfer, you can easily record the payment in Quicken.
- Quicken automatically matches payments to outstanding invoices, helping you track which invoices have been paid and which remain outstanding.
- You can link your **bank account** or **payment processing systems** (such as PayPal, Stripe, or Square) to automatically import payment transactions.

2. Tracking Payments and Deposits:

○ Quicken provides a **payment tracking** feature that enables you to log deposits as payments and link them to their corresponding invoices.

○ This ensures your records are up-to-date, preventing you from missing payments and helping you maintain a consistent cash flow.

Managing Business Expenses and Deductions

1. Tracking Business Expenses for Tax Deduction

One of the primary benefits of using Quicken for small business finance management is the ability to track business expenses efficiently. This is crucial not only for maintaining profitability but also for tax purposes. By accurately tracking your expenses, you can ensure that you claim all eligible tax deductions and reduce your tax liability at the end of the year.

2. How to Track Business Expenses

1. Entering Expense Transactions:

- In Quicken, you can manually enter your business expenses as they occur or sync them directly from your linked business accounts.
- Each expense can be categorized, ensuring that it is properly recorded under categories such as office supplies, marketing, utilities, or travel.

2. Managing Recurring Expenses:

- For expenses that recur monthly or annually (e.g., subscription services, rent, utilities), you can set up **recurring transactions** in Quicken.
- This automation saves you time and ensures that you don't forget to account for these recurring costs.

3. Identifying Tax-Deductible Expenses

1. **Tax Categories**:

   ○ Quicken allows you to assign **tax categories** to business expenses, such as:
     - Business mileage
     - Home office expenses
     - Travel expenses
     - Equipment and supplies
   ○ By categorizing your expenses correctly, Quicken can generate reports that show which expenses are eligible for tax deductions, making it easier for you to prepare your taxes.

2. **Tracking Mileage**:

   ○ For freelancers and small business owners who use their vehicle for business, Quicken has a built-in mileage tracker.
   ○ You can manually enter trips or set up automatic tracking to capture the mileage for business-related travel,

which is often deductible on your taxes.

3. **Using Quicken's Tax Reporting Features**:

   ○ Quicken can generate **tax-related reports** that outline your total deductible expenses for the year, simplifying the tax filing process and helping you ensure that you maximize your deductions.

Generating Profit and Loss Reports

1. Why Profit and Loss (P&L) Reports Matter

For any business, understanding your profit and loss (P&L) is crucial. This financial statement provides a snapshot of your revenue, expenses, and net profit over a specific period. By generating and reviewing P&L reports regularly, small business owners and freelancers can make informed decisions, set financial goals, and identify potential areas for improvement.

2. How to Generate Profit and Loss Reports in Quicken

1. **Creating a P&L Report**:

   - In Quicken, go to **Reports > Business > Profit & Loss**. You can select a date range, whether it's for the current month, quarter, or year.
   - Quicken will generate a detailed P&L report that includes:
     - Total income
     - Total business expenses
     - Net profit or loss
   - You can customize the report by filtering it by category, account, or vendor to see a breakdown of your financial performance.

2. **Reviewing P&L Insights**:

   - Quicken's P&L report allows you to see your income and expenses clearly, giving you an understanding of whether your business is profitable or if adjustments need to be made.

- o You can also track **net profit margins** and analyze trends over time.

3. **Exporting P&L Reports**:

- o Quicken allows you to export P&L reports into **Excel** or **PDF** formats, which can be shared with stakeholders, partners, or accountants.

Tax Planning and Preparation with Quicken

Tax season can be one of the most stressful times of the year for individuals and small business owners alike. With the complexity of tax laws, endless paperwork, and the potential for errors, managing taxes effectively can feel overwhelming. Fortunately, Quicken provides a comprehensive suite of tools to help you organize tax-related transactions, track deductions, and ensure that your tax preparation is as efficient and accurate as possible. By leveraging Quicken's features, you can reduce the stress associated with tax season, save valuable time, and make sure you're maximizing your tax benefits.

This section will guide you through the process of tax planning and preparation using Quicken, covering everything from organizing tax-related transactions to preparing for IRS audits. You will also learn how to track deductions, manage tax-advantaged accounts, and generate reports to export your data directly to tax software.

Organizing Tax-Related Transactions

1. Why Organizing Tax Transactions is Crucial

To ensure that you don't miss any valuable deductions or tax benefits, it is essential to keep track of your tax-related transactions throughout the year. Quicken allows you to categorize and track all your income and expenses, so they're ready when tax time arrives. Proper organization helps you avoid scrambling at the last minute, reduces the risk of missing tax breaks, and simplifies the process of filing your tax returns.

2. How to Organize Tax-Related Transactions in Quicken

1. **Categorizing Income and Expenses for Tax Purposes**:

   - **Income**: In Quicken, you can assign specific income categories that are relevant to your taxes, such as salary, freelance income, rental income, or investment income. This way, you can quickly access a summary of all your income streams for tax reporting purposes.
   - **Expenses**: Quicken allows you to create custom categories for business or personal expenses. For tax purposes, you'll want to separate out deductible expenses, such as business supplies, mileage, home office expenses, medical

expenses, charitable donations, and more.

2. **Using Tax Categories**: Quicken provides a set of predefined tax categories, such as:

   - **Business Expenses**: This includes things like office supplies, utilities, and other operating costs.
   - **Tax-Deductible Expenses**: These categories include medical expenses, home office deductions, and business mileage.
   - **Retirement Contributions**: Contributions to accounts like IRAs, 401(k)s, or other tax-deferred accounts.
   - You can also create **custom categories** to match your unique tax situation, ensuring that every expense is properly categorized.

3. **Tracking Tax Payments**: If you make estimated tax payments throughout the year, you can record them in Quicken to ensure they are accounted for when filing

your tax return. Quicken helps you track these payments by linking them to the relevant tax categories and allowing you to view them in your financial reports.

Tracking Deductions and Tax-Advantaged Accounts

1. Maximizing Deductions

One of the most powerful ways to reduce your tax liability is by maximizing your deductions. Quicken allows you to keep track of all tax-deductible expenses and helps you identify potential deductions that you might not otherwise consider.

2. Tracking Business Expenses for Deductions

If you're a small business owner or freelancer, you can use Quicken to track business expenses that are deductible, including:

- **Home Office**: If you use a portion of your home for your business, Quicken helps you track expenses like utilities, rent, mortgage interest, and property taxes that may be partially deductible.
- **Vehicle Mileage**: If you use your car for business purposes, you can use Quicken's mileage tracker to log trips and calculate your mileage deduction.
- **Office Supplies and Equipment**: Items like computers, software, printers, and office furniture may be deductible as business expenses.

3. Tracking Tax-Advantaged Accounts

In addition to business expenses, Quicken also helps you track contributions to tax-advantaged accounts, such as:

- **Retirement Accounts**: Quicken automatically tracks contributions to your 401(k), IRA, or other retirement accounts. You can easily categorize these contributions and generate reports to see how much you've contributed, ensuring that you're staying within contribution limits.

- **Health Savings Accounts (HSAs)**: Contributions to an HSA are tax-deductible, and Quicken makes it easy to track contributions and withdrawals, helping you take full advantage of this tax benefit.
- **529 College Savings Plans**: Quicken also tracks contributions to 529 plans, which offer tax advantages for saving for education.

By keeping detailed records of these accounts and contributions, Quicken ensures that you can easily report them during tax filing and maximize your deductions.

Generating Tax Reports and Exporting Data to Tax Software

1. Generating Tax Reports in Quicken

Quicken simplifies the tax preparation process by generating detailed reports that outline your income, expenses, and deductions, making it easy to identify your taxable income and eligible deductions. Here's how Quicken helps:

1. **Tax Summary Reports**:

   - Quicken can generate a **Tax Summary Report** that shows a comprehensive overview of your income and expenses for the year, categorized by tax category. This report helps you understand how much taxable income you have and which deductions you can claim.

2. **Tax-Deductible Expenses Report**:

   - For tax-deductible expenses, Quicken generates a **deductible expenses report** that details all qualifying expenses in categories like medical, charitable contributions, and business expenses. This report can help you determine exactly how much you can deduct.

3. **Retirement Contributions Report**:

○ Quicken generates a **retirement contribution report**, detailing all contributions to tax-deferred accounts. This report is particularly useful when you want to ensure you're staying within contribution limits and maximizing your retirement savings.

2. Exporting Data to Tax Software

Once you've generated your tax reports in Quicken, you can easily export the data to tax preparation software, such as TurboTax, H&R Block, or TaxSlayer, to simplify the filing process. Most major tax software programs integrate with Quicken, allowing you to:

● **Export Your Reports**: Quicken allows you to export your tax reports in a format compatible with most tax software programs. This means you don't have to manually input all your data into the tax software.

- **Automate Tax Filing**: By exporting your data, you can skip the tedious process of manually entering transactions, ensuring that your tax filings are accurate and up to date.
- **Track Refunds and Payments**: Quicken helps you track the status of your tax refund or balance due, so you can plan ahead for when your refund will arrive or when payments are due.

Preparing for IRS Audits and Keeping Digital Records

1. Why Digital Records Matter

Having accurate and organized records is crucial for defending yourself in the event of an IRS audit. Quicken ensures that all your transactions, tax deductions, and receipts are stored digitally and securely, which can help you provide the necessary documentation if requested by the IRS.

2. How to Use Quicken for Audit Preparation

1. **Detailed Transaction Records**:

   - Quicken keeps a detailed record of every transaction, including the date, amount, category, and vendor. This information can be crucial if you're ever audited by the IRS.
   - For every business expense, you can attach supporting documentation such as receipts or invoices. These can be stored digitally within Quicken or linked to your transactions.

2. **Tax Reports for Audit Defense**:

   - If you're audited, you can use Quicken's detailed tax reports to demonstrate how your expenses and income were calculated. Quicken generates reports that are easily understandable by both you and your accountant, which can help streamline the audit process.

3. **Document Management**:

   ○ Quicken allows you to attach and store digital copies of tax-related documents, such as receipts, invoices, and contracts. These documents can be attached to the corresponding transactions in Quicken for easy retrieval.
   ○ By keeping everything digital, you reduce the risk of losing important documents and ensure that you have everything you need in the event of an audit.

4. **Backup and Restore**:

   ○ Quicken allows you to back up your data regularly to an external drive or cloud storage, ensuring that your tax records are protected and easily accessible.

- This backup is essential in case your computer experiences any issues or you need to restore your financial data at a later time.

3. Maintaining Compliance and Avoiding Audits

1. **Avoiding Common Audit Triggers**:

   - The IRS uses specific triggers to determine which returns should be audited. Quicken helps you avoid common audit triggers by ensuring that your tax records are accurate and well-documented.
   - By categorizing all your transactions properly, keeping accurate records, and staying within the limits for deductions, you reduce the likelihood of an audit.

2. **Staying Informed About Tax Laws**:

○ Quicken regularly updates its software to reflect changes in tax laws, so you can stay compliant with the latest regulations. It helps ensure that you're claiming only valid deductions and that your tax filings are accurate.

Advanced Features and Customization

Quicken offers a robust array of advanced features and customization options designed to help users take full control of their finances. Whether you are looking for in-depth analysis through custom reports, streamlining your financial management across multiple devices, or automating repetitive tasks to save time, Quicken provides the tools necessary to elevate your financial planning and decision-making.

Creating and Customizing Reports for In-Depth Analysis

1. Why Custom Reports Matter

Reports are one of the most powerful features in Quicken. They allow you to analyze and visualize your financial data in a way that makes sense for your specific needs. Whether you're looking to assess your spending habits, track investment performance, or monitor your business's financial health, creating customized reports is essential to gaining an in-depth understanding of your finances.

Quicken allows you to create detailed, personalized reports that go beyond the basic templates, offering valuable insights that can inform your financial decisions. By customizing these reports, you can track specific areas of your finances that matter most to you, filter out irrelevant data, and highlight important trends.

2. How to Create Custom Reports

To create customized reports in Quicken, follow these steps:

1. **Choose a Report Type**:

   ○ Quicken offers a range of built-in report templates, such as spending reports, cash flow statements, tax reports, and investment performance reports. Choose the base report that most closely matches your goals.

2. **Filter and Tailor the Report**:

   ○ Once you've selected a report template, you can customize it by setting specific filters. For example, you can select the date range, the accounts, categories, or tags you want to include in the report.
   ○ You can also filter for certain transactions, such as business expenses, deductible costs, or specific income sources.

3. **Add or Remove Columns and Data**:

   ○ Quicken allows you to add or
     remove specific columns and fields
     in your reports. For example, if you
     need more detailed information
     about your expenses, you can
     include the vendor, payment
     method, or tags. If certain data isn't
     relevant, you can remove it to
     streamline your analysis.

4. **Format Your Report**:

   ○ Quicken lets you adjust the
     appearance of your reports. You can
     change the colors, font sizes, and
     layouts to make the report more
     visually appealing and easier to
     interpret.
   ○ You can also save your custom
     reports for future use, ensuring that
     you don't need to reconfigure them
     every time you run the report.

3. Examples of Advanced Reports

- **Net Worth Report**: Track your assets and liabilities to determine your financial health over time.
- **Investment Performance Report**: Monitor how your investments have performed by analyzing returns, dividends, and capital gains.
- **Expense vs. Income Report**: Compare your expenses against income to ensure you're sticking to your budget and identifying areas where you can save.
- **Cash Flow Projections**: Forecast your cash flow for the upcoming months based on historical data, helping you plan for future expenses.

Using Quicken on Multiple Devices and Cloud Syncing

1. The Importance of Multi-Device Access

In today's fast-paced world, it's important to access your financial data from multiple devices. Whether you're at home, at work, or on the go, Quicken offers a seamless experience across platforms. You can access your Quicken data from a desktop computer, laptop, and even a mobile device, ensuring you can always stay up-to-date with your finances.

2. Setting Up Cloud Syncing

Quicken supports cloud syncing, which allows you to access and update your financial data from multiple devices in real time. By syncing your Quicken data to the cloud, you ensure that all your devices have the most up-to-date information.

To set up cloud syncing in Quicken, follow these steps:

1. **Enable Cloud Syncing**:

   - On your desktop or laptop, go to the Quicken settings and enable cloud syncing. This will link your Quicken data to the Quicken Cloud, allowing it to be accessed from other devices.

2. **Download the Quicken Mobile App**:

   ○ If you want to access your data on the go, download the Quicken mobile app for iOS or Android. Once you've logged in with your Quicken account, the mobile app will sync your data from the cloud, giving you access to your financial information anywhere.

3. **Automatic Updates**:

   ○ Quicken automatically syncs your data to the cloud whenever changes are made, such as adding new transactions or editing existing ones. This ensures that your desktop, mobile, and cloud-based data are always in sync.

3. Benefits of Cloud Syncing

- **Access Anywhere**: Whether you're using a phone, tablet, or laptop, you can access your data and manage your finances without being tethered to one device.
- **Real-Time Updates**: When you update a transaction on your phone, it will immediately reflect on your desktop version and vice versa.
- **Data Security**: Your financial data is backed up to Quicken's secure cloud servers, minimizing the risk of losing your data if something happens to your device.

Setting Up and Using Custom Categories and Tags

1. Why Custom Categories and Tags are Essential

Quicken provides a broad set of predefined categories to help you organize your finances, but sometimes these categories are too general or not specific enough for your needs. This is where **custom categories** and **tags** come into play. Custom categories and tags allow you to organize your finances in a way that is highly personalized, ensuring that you can track exactly what's important to you.

- **Categories** are used to classify income and expenses in ways that make sense for your financial life (e.g., "Healthcare," "Entertainment," or "Client Expenses").
- **Tags** offer a secondary level of organization, allowing you to track specific details or themes, such as projects, trips, or even personal goals.

2. How to Create and Use Custom Categories

1. Create a Custom Category:

- To create a custom category, go to the "Categories" section in Quicken, select "New Category," and enter the name of your category. You can also assign it to a parent category (e.g., "Business" or "Personal") for better organization.

2. **Assign Categories to Transactions**:

    ○ When adding or editing a transaction, you can assign it to one of your custom categories. This allows you to quickly track and report on specific areas of your finances.

3. **Use Subcategories for More Granular Tracking**:

    ○ Quicken allows you to create subcategories under your main categories. For example, under "Business," you can create subcategories for "Client Payments," "Business Travel," or "Marketing Expenses."

3. How to Create and Use Tags

1. **Create a Tag**:

   ○ Similar to categories, you can
   create tags for specific purposes.
   For instance, you might want to
   track expenses related to a
   particular project, a trip, or an
   event.

2. **Assign Tags to Transactions**:

   ○ When entering or editing a
   transaction, simply add tags to it.
   You can assign multiple tags to a
   single transaction, giving you more
   flexibility in organizing your data.

3. **Filter Reports Using Tags**:

   ○ Tags allow you to filter and
   generate reports based on specific
   themes or objectives, such as
   monitoring a project's budget or
   tracking personal goals.

Automating Financial Tasks for Efficiency

1. Why Automation is Key to Financial Efficiency

One of the greatest benefits of using Quicken is its ability to automate time-consuming financial tasks. Automation allows you to set up recurring transactions, track bill payments, and even generate reports without having to manually update your data each time. By automating these processes, you can focus on higher-level financial planning and analysis.

2. Automating Bill Payments

Quicken's bill payment features allow you to set up automatic bill payments for regular expenses like utilities, subscriptions, and loans. Here's how you can automate your bill payments:

1. **Set Up Bill Reminders**:

   o Quicken will alert you when bills are due, allowing you to schedule payments in advance. You can specify the amount and frequency of the bill, ensuring that it's paid on time.

2. **Auto-Pay for Recurring Bills**:

   o You can set up automatic payments for recurring bills, so Quicken will pay them on your behalf. This ensures that you never miss a payment, and you won't have to manually process bills each month.

3. Automating Expense Tracking

1. **Download Transactions Automatically**:

   o You can connect your bank and credit card accounts to Quicken to automatically download transactions. This saves time by eliminating the need to manually input each transaction.

2. **Set Up Categorization Rules**:

○ Quicken allows you to create rules that automatically categorize transactions as they are downloaded. For example, all payments to your utility company could be automatically categorized as "Utilities."

4. Automating Reports

1. Schedule Regular Reports:

○ You can set up automated report generation in Quicken, so financial summaries or expense reports are created and sent to your email on a regular basis. This is especially useful for monitoring your spending or keeping track of investments without needing to run reports manually.

2. Automate Budget Tracking:

○ Set up automatic tracking of your budget, so Quicken can alert you

when you're approaching your
budget limits. This can be done
using Quicken's budgeting tool,
which automatically compares your
actual spending against your set
budget.

Troubleshooting and Common Issues

Quicken is a powerful financial management tool, but like any software, it can sometimes encounter technical issues. Whether you're dealing with connectivity problems, duplicate transactions, or software glitches, understanding how to troubleshoot and resolve common issues can help you get back on track quickly. In this section, we'll explore some of the most common issues users face with Quicken and provide practical solutions to fix them.

Fixing Bank Sync and Connection Problems

1. Why Bank Sync Issues Occur

One of the most valuable features of Quicken is its ability to sync with your bank and financial institutions, allowing for automatic transaction downloads. However, users occasionally face issues with syncing, such as transactions not downloading or account connections failing. Bank sync issues can occur due to several reasons, including:

- **Connection errors**: These occur when Quicken cannot establish a secure link with your bank.
- **Account or password changes**: If you've recently changed your bank account credentials or passwords, this could disrupt the connection.
- **Bank updates or system maintenance**: Banks sometimes perform system updates or maintenance that may temporarily disrupt the sync process.

- **Software bugs or outdated versions**:
Running outdated versions of Quicken
may cause compatibility issues with bank
connections.

2. Troubleshooting Bank Sync Issues

Here's how to resolve common bank sync
problems:

1. **Check for Quicken Updates**:

   - Ensure that you're running the
latest version of Quicken. Updates
often include fixes for compatibility
issues, including syncing problems
with financial institutions. You can
check for updates by going to the
"Help" menu and selecting "Check
for Updates."

2. **Reauthorize the Account Connection**:

   - If your bank account is no longer
syncing, you might need to
reauthorize the connection. To do

this, go to the "Accounts" section, select the bank account, and choose "Edit Account Details." From there, you can reconnect the account by entering your login credentials again.

3. **Verify Your Bank's Online Services**:

   ○ Confirm that your bank's online banking services are operational and that they support Quicken's download functionality. Check your bank's website for any notices about outages or system maintenance.

4. **Refresh the Connection**:

   ○ If you're having trouble syncing, try refreshing the connection by clicking on "Update Now" or "Sync Now" in Quicken's banking or transactions section. This can prompt Quicken to reattempt downloading your transactions.

5. **Check Your Internet Connection**:

   ○ Ensure that you have a stable and
   reliable internet connection, as a
   weak or intermittent connection
   could interfere with the syncing
   process.

6. **Contact Customer Support**:

   ○ If you've tried all of the above and
   the issue persists, contact Quicken
   customer support for assistance.
   They may be able to diagnose the
   problem and offer a more specific
   solution.

Handling Duplicate Transactions and Errors

1. Why Duplicate Transactions Occur

Duplicate transactions are a common issue for
Quicken users, and they can occur for several
reasons:

- **Automatic downloads from the bank**: When Quicken automatically downloads transactions, it may accidentally import the same transaction multiple times if there are synchronization issues or conflicting data from the bank.
- **Manual entry errors**: Sometimes, users may manually enter a transaction that was already downloaded from the bank, resulting in duplicates.
- **Account reconciliation mistakes**: When reconciling accounts, a mismatch between the bank's records and the Quicken records can cause transactions to be duplicated.

2. Troubleshooting Duplicate Transactions

Follow these steps to resolve duplicate transaction issues:

1. **Use Quicken's Duplicate Transaction Detection Tool**:

- Quicken has an automatic duplicate transaction detection feature that can help identify and remove duplicates. You can access this tool by selecting "Edit" and then "Find and Recategorize" or "Find Duplicate Transactions." Quicken will highlight duplicate entries, and you can choose to delete or merge them.

2. **Manually Delete Duplicates**:

- If Quicken does not automatically detect duplicates, you can manually identify and delete them. To do this, go to the transaction list, right-click on the duplicate transaction, and select "Delete" or "Delete Transaction."

3. **Check for Double Downloads**:

- Sometimes, Quicken may download the same transaction twice, especially if you have multiple

accounts linked to the same
financial institution. To resolve this,
make sure you are downloading
transactions only once per account.
Double-check the download
settings in the "Banking" section of
Quicken.

4. **Review Bank Connection Settings**:

   o If duplicate transactions continue to
      appear, it may be due to a
      misconfigured account connection.
      Verify the account settings to ensure
      that the connection is properly set
      up, and ensure that Quicken isn't
      downloading the same data from
      multiple sources.

5. **Reconcile Your Accounts**:

   o Reconcile your bank accounts in
      Quicken to identify any
      discrepancies. This helps ensure
      that all transactions are accounted

for and that there are no errors in your transaction history.

Restoring Backups and Recovering Lost Data

1. Why You Might Need to Restore Backups

Sometimes, users may accidentally delete important financial data or encounter a software crash that results in data loss. Quicken offers a backup feature that automatically saves your financial data, which can be restored in the event of data loss, system failure, or user error. Here are some common scenarios that may require restoring a backup:

- **Accidental file deletion**: You may accidentally delete or overwrite your Quicken file.
- **Software crashes or data corruption**: Quicken files may become corrupted due to software errors or system issues.

- **Reinstalling Quicken**: If you need to reinstall Quicken due to a fresh system setup or software issue, restoring a backup will help you avoid losing your financial data.

2. How to Restore Backups

1. **Restore from Automatic Backups**:

    ○ Quicken automatically creates backup files at regular intervals. To restore from a recent backup, follow these steps:
    1. Open Quicken.
    2. Select "File" from the top menu.
    3. Choose "Restore a Backup File" from the drop-down menu.
    4. Browse through your backups and select the one you want to restore.

5. Follow the on-screen instructions to complete the restoration process.

2. **Restore from a Manual Backup**:

   o If you've manually backed up your Quicken data (for example, to an external drive or cloud storage), you can restore your data by selecting the backup file and following the same process outlined above.

3. **Verify Data Integrity**:

   o After restoring a backup, verify that all your data has been correctly restored and that no information has been lost. Reconcile your accounts to ensure that all transactions are accurate.

Dealing with Software Updates and Compatibility Issues

1. Why Software Updates Matter

Software updates are essential for keeping Quicken running smoothly and securely. Updates can fix bugs, add new features, improve performance, and ensure compatibility with the latest operating systems and financial institutions. However, sometimes updates can cause issues, particularly if there are compatibility problems with your operating system or if the update itself has a bug.

2. Troubleshooting Software Update Issues

1. **Ensure Your System Meets the Requirements**:

   ○ Before updating Quicken, make sure your computer meets the system requirements for the latest version of the software. Quicken updates often require newer versions of Windows or macOS, so check the system requirements before proceeding with the update.

2. **Check for Update Notifications**:

   o Quicken will typically notify you when an update is available. If you're experiencing issues, go to the "Help" menu and select "Check for Updates" to see if an update is available. Install the update and restart the software.

3. **Resolve Compatibility Issues**:

   o If you encounter problems after installing a software update, it might be due to compatibility issues with your operating system. In this case, try the following:

      ■ **Update Your Operating System**: Make sure you are running the latest version of Windows or macOS, as older versions may not be

compatible with the latest
version of Quicken.

- **Reinstall Quicken**: If an
update causes issues, try
uninstalling and reinstalling
Quicken to ensure the
installation is clean.

4. **Check for Bug Fixes and Patches**:

   ○ Occasionally, Quicken releases
   patches or bug fixes to address
   specific issues introduced by an
   update. Check Quicken's support
   site for any available patches that
   might fix the problems you're
   experiencing.

5. **Contact Quicken Support**:

   ○ If you're still having trouble after
   updating Quicken or encountering
   issues with software compatibility,
   contact Quicken support for
   assistance. They can help you
   troubleshoot the issue and provide

solutions based on your specific situation.

Expert Tips, Tricks, and Hidden Features

As you become more proficient with Quicken, you may start to uncover advanced tips and tricks that can significantly enhance your financial management experience. From speeding up data entry to customizing reports and syncing with third-party tools, there are numerous ways to unlock Quicken's full potential. This section will guide you through expert tips, shortcuts, hidden features, and best practices for maximizing Quicken's power.

Power User Tips for Faster Data Entry

One of the most important aspects of using Quicken effectively is data entry. The more time-efficient you are at entering your financial transactions, the more streamlined your workflow becomes. Here are some expert tips for speeding up the process:

1. Use the "QuickFill" Feature

Quicken's "QuickFill" feature is designed to automatically complete information for transactions based on your previous entries. For example, if you frequently make payments to a particular vendor, Quicken will prefill the transaction details such as the payee's name, amount, and category. This can save a lot of time when entering routine transactions.

To use QuickFill, just start typing the first few letters of the payee or category, and Quicken will present suggestions based on your history. If it's the transaction you want, simply press "Enter" to auto-fill the rest of the details.

2. Use the "Auto-Entry" Feature for Recurring Transactions

If you have recurring bills or income, such as a monthly rent payment or salary, Quicken can automatically enter these transactions for you. You can set up recurring transactions in Quicken by selecting "Tools" from the menu, then "Manage Bills & Income." Once set up, Quicken will automatically enter these transactions in your account every month, allowing you to avoid repetitive data entry.

3. Utilize Memorized Transactions

If you often deal with similar transactions (like utilities or subscription payments), memorizing them can save you time. Quicken allows you to create a list of memorized transactions, which can be automatically inserted into your transaction list with just a few clicks. To memorize a transaction, simply enter it manually, and then select "Memorize Transaction" from the transaction window.

4. Import Transactions from Your Bank

To minimize manual data entry, Quicken lets you import transactions directly from your bank or credit card account. The software supports direct downloads from thousands of institutions, making it easy to import transactions automatically rather than entering them by hand. Be sure to regularly sync your accounts to ensure the latest transactions are imported into Quicken.

5. Use Split Transactions for Complex Entries

For more complex expenses, such as a payment for a dinner bill that includes both meals and tax, Quicken allows you to split transactions across different categories. This lets you accurately track various types of expenses within a single entry. To split a transaction, simply select "Split" when entering the transaction and choose the different categories that apply.

Shortcuts and Customization Hacks

Quicken comes with several shortcuts and customization options that can make navigation and management faster and more efficient. Mastering these features will help you save time and access key functions quickly.

1. Keyboard Shortcuts

Using keyboard shortcuts in Quicken can drastically speed up your workflow. Here are some essential shortcuts to remember:

- **Ctrl + I** – Enter a new transaction
- **Ctrl + T** – Open the "Enter Transaction" window
- **Ctrl + R** – Reconcile your accounts
- **Ctrl + M** – Memorize a transaction
- **Ctrl + F** – Open the "Find and Replace" search function
- **Ctrl + E** – Edit a transaction
- **Ctrl + Shift + R** – Refresh your data and sync online

- **Ctrl + B** – Open the "Bill Manager" to view and pay bills

2. Customizing the Dashboard for Quick Access

The Quicken dashboard is fully customizable, allowing you to prioritize the information that matters most to you. You can add or remove widgets and adjust the layout to suit your needs. For example, you can display charts that track your budget, investments, or net worth in real time. To customize the dashboard, click on the gear icon in the top-right corner of the dashboard and select "Customize."

3. Customizing Categories and Tags

For more detailed financial tracking, you can customize categories and tags in Quicken. Categories help you organize transactions into groups (e.g., "Utilities" or "Groceries"), while tags allow you to label specific transactions for easier tracking. You can modify these categories and tags by going to the "Tools" menu, selecting

"Category List," and adding or editing categories to fit your financial goals.

4. Creating Custom Reports

Quicken lets you create custom reports that provide in-depth insights into your spending, income, or investment performance. You can filter reports based on specific categories, dates, or accounts. To create a custom report, go to "Reports" in the menu, select "Customize," and modify the report settings to suit your needs. You can even save your custom reports for future use.

5. Adjusting Default Preferences

Quicken offers a range of default preferences that control how the software behaves, from the way transactions are categorized to how reports are displayed. You can fine-tune these preferences to match your financial habits. To adjust preferences, go to "Edit" in the menu, select "Preferences," and review the settings for things like online banking, transaction entry, and report generation.

Using Quicken with Third-Party Tools and Apps

One of the key strengths of Quicken is its ability to integrate with a variety of third-party tools and applications. By leveraging these integrations, you can expand Quicken's functionality and better streamline your financial management process.

1. Integrating with Online Banking and Payment Services

Quicken allows you to link and sync your accounts with a range of banks and financial institutions. Many banks support direct downloading of transactions into Quicken, which helps automate data entry and ensures your records are always up to date. Additionally, Quicken works seamlessly with services like

PayPal and Venmo for managing e-commerce transactions, giving you an all-in-one view of your finances.

2. Using Quicken with Tax Software

Quicken's tax-related features are robust, but you can enhance your tax planning and filing process by integrating Quicken with tax preparation software such as TurboTax. This allows you to export your financial data directly into the software, making the process of filing taxes easier and reducing the risk of errors. To export your data, go to "File," select "Export," and choose the tax software you use.

3. Connecting with Investment Tools

For users who invest regularly, Quicken integrates with investment tracking tools like Morningstar and other portfolio management apps. By linking these third-party apps to Quicken, you can get a more comprehensive overview of your investments and track your portfolio performance across different platforms.

Quicken's ability to import investment transactions makes it easier to stay on top of gains, losses, and dividends.

4. Using Quicken with Budgeting Apps

Quicken's budgeting features are powerful, but some users may prefer using a dedicated budgeting tool in combination with Quicken. Apps like Mint or You Need a Budget (YNAB) can sync with Quicken, allowing for more granular budgeting while still using Quicken to track expenses, bills, and investments. Integration between these apps ensures a smooth workflow across all aspects of your financial life.

Security and Privacy Best Practices

As Quicken holds sensitive financial data, it's crucial to implement best practices for security and privacy. By following these guidelines, you can keep your data safe and secure from unauthorized access.

1. Use Strong Passwords and Two-Factor Authentication

The first line of defense for your Quicken account is a strong password. Ensure your password is unique and contains a combination of letters, numbers, and symbols. Additionally, enable two-factor authentication (2FA) whenever possible. This adds an extra layer of security by requiring a verification code in addition to your password when logging in.

2. Regularly Backup Your Data

Backing up your Quicken data regularly is crucial in case of system failure, data corruption, or accidental deletion. You can back up your data to an external hard drive, cloud storage, or a secure network. Quicken offers automatic backup options that you can configure under the "Backup" settings, but it's a good idea to perform manual backups periodically as well.

3. Use Encryption for Sensitive Data

When storing your Quicken data on your computer or in the cloud, always use encryption to protect sensitive information. Quicken allows you to set up a password for your data file, ensuring that only you can access it. For added security, enable encryption for any backups you create to further protect your financial information.

4. Keep Your Software and Operating System Updated

Security vulnerabilities in outdated software are a prime target for hackers. Always update Quicken to the latest version and ensure your operating system has the latest security patches installed. Quicken automatically checks for updates, but you can manually check by going to "Help" and selecting "Check for Updates."

5. Avoid Public Wi-Fi for Financial Transactions

Public Wi-Fi networks are inherently insecure, making them an easy target for cybercriminals. Always avoid accessing your Quicken data or conducting financial transactions over public Wi-Fi. If you must use public Wi-Fi, consider using a VPN (Virtual Private Network) to encrypt your internet connection.

6. Monitor Your Accounts Regularly

Regularly review your bank accounts, credit cards, and other financial accounts to ensure there are no unauthorized transactions. Quicken makes it easy to monitor all of your accounts in one place, so use this feature to spot any discrepancies early.

Case Studies: Real-Life Applications of Quicken

Quicken is more than just a financial management tool—it is a powerful system that transforms how individuals and businesses handle their finances. The following real-life case studies illustrate how different users have leveraged Quicken's features to overcome financial challenges, optimize their budgeting, and achieve their long-term financial goals.

Case Study 1: How a Freelancer Streamlined Income and Expenses

Background

Michael Simmons, a 34-year-old freelance graphic designer, struggled with inconsistent income and unpredictable expenses. Unlike salaried employees, his income varied significantly from month to month, making budgeting, tax preparation, and financial planning difficult. Michael often found himself scrambling to pay bills in low-income months and had difficulty tracking business-related expenses for tax deductions.

Challenges

1. **Inconsistent cash flow:** Michael's income fluctuated based on the number of client projects.
2. **Tracking business and personal expenses separately:** Without a structured system, he mixed personal and

business expenses, making tax season
stressful.

3. **Saving for taxes and emergencies:** He
   lacked a clear plan to set aside money for
   quarterly tax payments and unexpected
   expenses.

How Quicken Helped

1. **Setting Up Business and Personal
   Accounts:**
   Michael used Quicken Home & Business
   to separate his personal and business
   finances. He linked his business bank
   account, PayPal, and credit card to track
   income and expenses automatically.

2. **Tracking Client Payments and Invoices:**
   Quicken allowed Michael to generate and
   track invoices. He set up payment
   reminders to follow up on overdue
   invoices, ensuring a steady cash flow.

3. **Expense Categorization for Tax
   Deductions:**

By categorizing expenses (e.g., software subscriptions, office supplies, travel expenses), he could easily identify deductible business costs, saving him thousands in taxes.

4. **Creating an Emergency Fund and Tax Savings Plan:**
   Michael set up an automated savings plan in Quicken, allocating 25% of each payment received into a tax savings account and another 10% into an emergency fund.

Results

- Reduced financial stress by ensuring he had funds set aside for taxes.
- Streamlined invoice tracking and improved cash flow by reducing unpaid invoices.
- Maximized tax deductions, leading to significant savings.

- Built a stable financial cushion to handle low-income months.

Case Study 2: A Small Business Owner's Journey to Financial Clarity

Background

Karen Douglas, a 48-year-old owner of a boutique marketing agency, struggled with managing her business's growing financial needs. She had multiple revenue streams, recurring expenses, and employees to pay. As her company expanded, tracking cash flow, payroll, and profitability became increasingly complex.

Challenges

1. **Lack of financial visibility:** Karen had trouble understanding where her money was going each month.

2. **Payroll management:** As her team grew, managing payroll expenses manually became cumbersome.

3. **Budgeting and forecasting:** Without clear financial insights, planning for future expenses was difficult.

How Quicken Helped

1. **Tracking Income and Expenses with Business Reports:**
   Karen used Quicken's Profit & Loss reports to analyze her agency's revenue and expenses in real-time, helping her identify where to cut costs and reinvest profits.

2. **Managing Payroll Efficiently:**
   She integrated Quicken with her payroll provider, automating salary payments and tax withholdings.

3. **Budgeting and Forecasting Growth:**
   With Quicken's forecasting tools, Karen set revenue goals and allocated funds for

marketing, hiring, and office expansion.

4. **Tax Preparation and Compliance:**
   Quicken simplified her tax preparation by generating reports on deductible expenses, ensuring she stayed compliant with IRS regulations.

Results

- Gained a clear understanding of her business's financial health.
- Streamlined payroll processing, saving time and reducing errors.
- Improved cash flow management, ensuring funds were available for growth initiatives.
- Successfully expanded her team and office space based on accurate financial projections.

Case Study 3: How a Retiree Used Quicken to Manage Investments and Retirement Planning

Background

James and Patricia Mitchell, a retired couple in their late 60s, faced challenges in managing their multiple retirement income sources, investment accounts, and daily expenses. With pensions, Social Security, and investment dividends, they needed a way to track their income and ensure their nest egg lasted throughout retirement.

Challenges

1. **Tracking multiple income streams:** The couple had income from Social Security, pensions, annuities, and investments, making financial tracking complex.
2. **Managing investment portfolios:** They struggled with understanding how their retirement funds were performing.

3. **Ensuring sustainable withdrawals:**
   They needed to budget withdrawals to
   avoid depleting their savings.

How Quicken Helped

1. **Consolidating Retirement Accounts in
   One View:**
   Quicken allowed James and Patricia to
   link their retirement and investment
   accounts, giving them a real-time view of
   their assets.

2. **Tracking Investment Performance and
   Dividends:**
   Using Quicken's investment tracking
   features, they monitored their stock and
   bond portfolios, ensuring their
   investments were aligned with their risk
   tolerance and retirement goals.

3. **Budgeting for Fixed and Variable
   Expenses:**
   They created a retirement budget,
   allocating funds for fixed expenses

(mortgage, utilities) and discretionary spending (travel, dining).

4. **Sustainable Withdrawal Strategy:**
   Quicken helped them plan a safe withdrawal rate, ensuring they wouldn't outlive their savings.

Results

- Achieved financial peace of mind by tracking all income and expenses in one place.
- Improved investment decision-making, optimizing their retirement portfolio.
- Successfully maintained a withdrawal strategy that ensured long-term financial stability.
- Gained confidence in their ability to manage money in retirement.

Case Study 4: A Family's Story – Budgeting for Long-Term Financial Success

Background

Luis and Maria Martinez, a couple in their 40s with two children, faced difficulties in managing household expenses, saving for their kids' education, and planning for homeownership. Despite steady incomes, they often found themselves short on savings due to untracked expenses.

Challenges

1. **Uncontrolled spending:** The family lacked visibility into where their money was going.
2. **Struggles with saving for education and homeownership:** They needed a structured plan to achieve their financial goals.
3. **Difficulty in tracking monthly bills and due dates:** Late payments led to unnecessary fees.

How Quicken Helped

1. **Setting Up a Family Budget:**
   Luis and Maria used Quicken's budgeting tools to categorize expenses, track spending, and adjust their habits.

2. **Automating Bill Payments and Alerts:**
   They set up Quicken's bill reminders, ensuring they never missed a payment and avoided late fees.

3. **Establishing Savings Goals:**
   They created savings categories for their children's college fund and a future home down payment, automating monthly contributions.

4. **Analyzing Spending Trends Over Time:**
   With Quicken's reports and charts, they identified unnecessary expenses and reallocated funds toward savings.

Results

- Built a structured household budget that reduced financial stress.
- Saved consistently for major life goals, including homeownership and education.
- Avoided late fees and improved credit scores through automated bill payments.
- Gained financial confidence and stability for their family's future.

Bonus Resources and Companion Tools

Mastering Quicken is not just about learning the software—it's about integrating the best practices and additional tools to streamline your financial management process. This section provides valuable companion resources, recommended books and tools, online communities, and strategies for staying updated with Quicken's latest features. These resources will help you optimize your financial planning, troubleshoot issues efficiently, and continually improve your skills.

Recommended Financial Planning Books and Tools

Beyond Quicken, there are several excellent books and tools that can enhance your financial knowledge and help you develop better money management habits. Below are some of the best resources that complement your use of Quicken.

1. Personal Finance and Budgeting Books

- **"The Total Money Makeover" by Dave Ramsey** – A step-by-step plan for managing debt, budgeting effectively, and achieving financial independence.
- **"Your Money or Your Life" by Vicki Robin and Joe Dominguez** – A transformative guide to understanding financial freedom and aligning money with personal values.
- **"The Millionaire Next Door" by Thomas J. Stanley and William D. Danko** – Research-based insights into how everyday individuals build wealth over time.

- **"I Will Teach You to Be Rich" by Ramit Sethi** – A modern, actionable guide to automating finances and growing wealth.

2. Investment and Retirement Planning Books

- **"The Intelligent Investor" by Benjamin Graham** – A classic book on value investing and long-term financial success.
- **"The Little Book of Common Sense Investing" by John C. Bogle** – A guide to passive investing and index funds from the founder of Vanguard.
- **"Retire Before Mom and Dad" by Rob Berger** – A step-by-step approach to achieving financial independence through smart investment strategies.

3. Companion Financial Tools

- **YNAB (You Need a Budget)** – A budgeting tool that can complement Quicken by focusing on cash flow and envelope budgeting.

- **Personal Capital** – A free investment and net worth tracking tool that provides an additional perspective on your portfolio.
- **TurboTax** – A leading tax preparation software that integrates with Quicken for easy tax filing.
- **Evernote or Notion** – Great tools for storing financial documents, receipts, and notes related to your finances.

Best Online Communities and Forums for Quicken Users

Being part of an active community can significantly enhance your learning experience with Quicken. Online forums and discussion groups allow users to ask questions, share troubleshooting tips, and discover hidden features.

1. Quicken Official Community Forum

- Hosted by Quicken itself, this is the best place to get official support, software updates, and expert advice.
- Website: https://community.quicken.com

2. Reddit – r/Quicken

- A user-driven subreddit where Quicken users discuss troubleshooting tips, feature requests, and financial best practices.
- Website: https://www.reddit.com/r/Quicken

3. Bogleheads Forum

- A community focused on personal finance and investing, with dedicated discussions on financial software like Quicken.
- Website: https://www.bogleheads.org/forum

4. Facebook Groups for Quicken Users

- Several private and public Facebook groups where users share experiences, tips, and best practices.

- Examples: **Quicken Tips & Tricks, Quicken Users Help & Support**

5. Stack Exchange – Personal Finance & Money

- A Q&A platform where finance professionals and tech-savvy Quicken users provide detailed answers to common problems.
- Website: https://money.stackexchange.com

Being an active participant in these communities allows you to stay updated with Quicken's latest developments, troubleshoot issues quickly, and learn best practices from seasoned users.

Ongoing Learning: How to Stay Updated with Quicken Changes

Quicken regularly updates its software to add new features, improve security, and enhance user experience. Staying informed about these updates ensures that you're leveraging the latest improvements and maintaining smooth financial management.

1. Follow Quicken's Official Blog and Announcements

- Quicken's official blog and announcements page provide information on new features, security updates, and software improvements.
- Website: https://www.quicken.com/blog

2. Subscribe to Quicken's YouTube Channel

- The Quicken YouTube channel offers tutorials, webinars, and feature breakdowns for both beginners and advanced users.
- Website: https://www.youtube.com/user/Quicken

3. Take Online Courses and Webinars

- Platforms like **Udemy**, **Skillshare**, and **LinkedIn Learning** offer Quicken tutorials that cover advanced features and real-world applications.

- Many of these courses are updated as new versions of Quicken are released.

4. Read Industry News and Financial Blogs

- Websites like **Investopedia**, **NerdWallet**, and **The Motley Fool** regularly cover personal finance and financial software updates.
- Following these sites helps users stay informed about trends that may impact their use of Quicken.

5. Join Beta Testing Programs

- Quicken occasionally offers beta testing programs for users who want early access to new features and are willing to provide feedback.
- Interested users can apply through Quicken's community forum.

6. Enable Automatic Updates in Quicken

- Ensure that your Quicken software is set
  to receive automatic updates so you
  always have the latest features and
  security patches.

Conclusion

Managing personal and business finances can often feel overwhelming, but with the right tools, strategies, and mindset, financial control is within reach. Throughout this book, we have explored the full potential of Quicken, from setting up accounts and tracking expenses to mastering advanced features like investment management and tax planning. Now that you have gained in-depth knowledge of how to use Quicken effectively, it's time to take the next steps toward financial mastery.

Final Thoughts and Next Steps

Quicken is more than just a budgeting tool—it's a comprehensive financial management system designed to help you take control of your money, minimize stress, and plan for the future. Whether you're using Quicken for personal budgeting, running a small business, or managing retirement investments, the key to success is **consistent engagement and financial awareness**.

Now that you have completed this book, here are the key takeaways to guide you forward:

1. **Financial Awareness Leads to Better Decision-Making**

   o Regularly updating and reviewing your Quicken data helps you understand your financial habits.
   o Awareness of income and expenses allows you to make informed financial choices.
   o The insights gained from Quicken reports can help you set realistic financial goals.

2. **Automation Saves Time and Reduces Stress**

   - ○ Setting up **automated bill payments, recurring transactions, and alerts** ensures that you stay on top of your finances effortlessly.
   - ○ Using Quicken's auto-categorization and bank sync features minimizes manual data entry.
   - ○ By streamlining your financial tasks, you free up time to focus on long-term financial planning.

3. **Budgeting and Expense Tracking Are the Foundations of Financial Stability**

   - ○ Sticking to a **realistic budget** prevents unnecessary spending and builds healthy financial habits.
   - ○ Tracking expenses diligently ensures that your spending aligns with your financial goals.

- Adjusting your budget as life circumstances change helps maintain long-term financial stability.

4. **Investing and Retirement Planning Require Ongoing Monitoring**

   - Whether you are managing stocks, mutual funds, or retirement accounts, regular **portfolio reviews** are essential.
   - Quicken's investment tracking features help you evaluate your risk exposure and diversify your assets.
   - Planning ahead for **retirement, tax obligations, and wealth accumulation** ensures financial security in the future.

5. **Ongoing Learning Enhances Financial Mastery**

   - Staying updated with **Quicken's latest features** ensures you get the most out of the software.

- Joining online financial communities, reading finance books, and using companion tools can help you refine your financial skills.
- Learning about **new tax laws, investment strategies, and budgeting methods** will keep you ahead of financial challenges.

At this stage, the next step is to **take action**. Knowledge alone is not enough; applying what you've learned will make all the difference. Start implementing the best practices covered in this book, set up your financial goals in Quicken, and commit to regularly maintaining your financial records.

Staying Committed to Financial Success

Financial success is not a one-time achievement—it's an ongoing process that requires discipline, consistency, and adaptability.

Many people start strong but gradually fall back into poor financial habits due to a lack of commitment. The key to long-term success is to integrate **financial management into your routine** and make it a natural part of your life.

1. Establish a Routine for Managing Your Finances

To avoid financial mismanagement, set up a consistent schedule for reviewing and updating your Quicken data:

- **Daily:** Quickly review transactions and ensure everything is categorized correctly.
- **Weekly:** Check your budget, monitor upcoming bill payments, and review financial goals.
- **Monthly:** Reconcile bank transactions, analyze cash flow reports, and make necessary budget adjustments.
- **Quarterly:** Review investment performance, tax obligations, and savings goals.

- **Annually:** Evaluate your overall financial health, set new financial goals, and prepare for tax season.

2. Regularly Adjust Your Financial Goals

As life evolves, so do your financial needs. Major events like a career change, marriage, starting a business, or retirement will require adjustments to your financial strategy.

- Use Quicken's **goal-setting tools** to track your progress.
- Periodically revisit your **savings, debt reduction, and investment goals** to ensure they align with your current financial situation.
- Adjust your **budget and spending habits** as needed to maintain financial stability.

3. Keep Learning and Improving

Financial education never stops. Stay ahead of financial challenges by continuously improving your knowledge:

- Follow **Quicken's official updates** to stay informed about new features.
- Read **personal finance books and blogs** to learn about new budgeting and investment strategies.
- Join **online forums and communities** where you can engage with other Quicken users and share best practices.

4. Stay Motivated by Tracking Your Progress

It's easy to lose motivation when financial progress seems slow. Keep yourself motivated by:

- **Setting short-term milestones** (e.g., paying off a credit card, saving a certain amount).
- **Celebrating financial wins** (e.g., reducing debt, increasing savings, hitting investment targets).
- **Reviewing reports in Quicken** to see how far you've come and where improvements can be made.

Where to Get Help and Support

No matter how proficient you become with Quicken, there may be times when you need additional support. Fortunately, there are plenty of **resources** available to help you troubleshoot problems, learn advanced features, and connect with other Quicken users.

1. Quicken Official Support

If you encounter technical issues or need assistance with software functionality, Quicken's official support team can provide direct help.

- **Website:** https://www.quicken.com/support
- **Phone Support:** Available for Quicken users with an active subscription.
- **Live Chat:** Instant messaging support available on the Quicken website.

2. Quicken Community Forums

A vibrant online community where users discuss troubleshooting tips, share experiences, and exchange best practices.

- **Website:** https://community.quicken.com
- **Best for:** Common troubleshooting solutions, feature discussions, and peer-to-peer advice.

3. Online Learning Platforms and Tutorials

For those who prefer step-by-step tutorials, video lessons, and online courses, these platforms can be valuable:

- **YouTube** – Many Quicken experts share tutorials on advanced features.
- **Udemy** – Offers in-depth courses on Quicken, including financial management strategies.
- **Skillshare** – Features finance courses that complement Quicken's budgeting and investment tools.

4. Social Media Groups and Reddit Communities

Engaging with other Quicken users on social media can be a great way to stay informed about updates and solutions.

- **Reddit:** https://www.reddit.com/r/Quicken
- **Facebook Groups:** Search for "Quicken Users Help & Support" for active discussions.

5. Financial Advisors and Accountants

If you require more **personalized financial advice**, consulting a **certified financial planner (CFP)** or accountant can help you optimize your use of Quicken for complex financial needs such as tax planning, investment strategies, and small business management.

Glossary of Terms

A

- **Account Register** – A digital ledger in Quicken where all transactions related to a specific account (bank, credit card, investment, etc.) are recorded.
- **Allocation** – The process of distributing income, expenses, or investments across different categories or accounts.
- **Amortization** – The gradual reduction of a debt over time through scheduled payments that cover both interest and principal.
- **Asset Allocation** – The distribution of investments among different asset classes

(stocks, bonds, real estate, etc.) to balance risk and reward.

- **Auto-Categorization** – A Quicken feature that automatically assigns categories to imported transactions based on past behavior.
- **Automatic Backup** – A feature in Quicken that saves copies of your financial data to prevent loss.
- **Automatic Bill Pay** – A feature that allows users to schedule and automate recurring payments for bills.

B

- **Balance Sheet** – A financial statement that summarizes assets, liabilities, and net worth at a given point in time.
- **Bank Reconciliation** – The process of matching transactions recorded in Quicken with bank statements to ensure accuracy.

- **Bill Manager** – Quicken's built-in tool for tracking and paying bills.
- **Budgeting** – The process of creating a financial plan that allocates income toward expenses, savings, and investments.
- **Business Expenses** – Costs incurred by a business that can be deducted from taxable income.

C

- **Capital Gains** – The profit earned from selling an investment at a higher price than the purchase price.
- **Cash Flow** – The movement of money into (income) and out of (expenses) a person's or business's accounts.
- **Check Register** – A digital or physical record of checks written, deposits made, and transactions completed.

- **Cloud Syncing** – A Quicken feature that allows users to sync their financial data across multiple devices.
- **Credit Limit** – The maximum amount of money a borrower can charge on a credit account.
- **Currency Exchange Rate** – The value of one currency in terms of another, relevant for international transactions.
- **Custom Categories** – User-defined categories in Quicken for more personalized financial tracking.

D

- **Debt-to-Income Ratio (DTI)** – A measure of how much of a person's income is used to pay off debt.
- **Depreciation** – The reduction in value of an asset over time, often used for tax deductions.

- **Direct Connect** – A method for linking Quicken with financial institutions to automatically download transactions.
- **Dividend** – A portion of a company's earnings paid to shareholders.
- **Duplicate Transaction** – An error in which a transaction appears more than once in an account register.

E

- **Electronic Funds Transfer (EFT)** – A method of electronically moving money from one account to another.
- **Emergency Fund** – A savings account used for unexpected expenses or financial emergencies.
- **Encryption** – A security feature in Quicken that protects financial data from unauthorized access.
- **Equity** – The ownership value of an asset after subtracting liabilities.

- **Estimated Taxes** – Quarterly tax payments required for self-employed individuals and businesses.
- **Expense Report** – A summary of spending in various categories over a given period.

F

- **Financial Statement** – A document that provides an overview of financial activities, including balance sheets and income statements.
- **Fixed Expenses** – Regular expenses that remain consistent, such as rent or mortgage payments.
- **Floating Transactions** – Transactions that have been entered but not yet cleared by the bank.
- **Forecasting** – The process of predicting future financial trends based on historical data.

- **Fraud Alert** – A security feature that notifies users of potential unauthorized transactions.

G

- **Gross Income** – The total income earned before taxes and deductions.
- **Goal Tracking** – A Quicken feature that helps users set and monitor financial goals such as saving for a house or paying off debt.

H

- **Home & Business Edition** – A version of Quicken tailored for users who need both personal and business financial tracking.

I

- **Importing Transactions** – The process of downloading and adding financial transactions from a bank or credit card account into Quicken.
- **Income Statement** – A report showing revenue, expenses, and profit or loss over a specific period.
- **Interest Rate** – The percentage charged or earned on loans, credit, or investments.
- **Investment Portfolio** – A collection of financial assets such as stocks, bonds, and real estate.
- **IRA (Individual Retirement Account)** – A tax-advantaged retirement savings account.

J

- **Journal Entry** – A manual financial entry used for recording transactions, often in accounting software.

L

- **Liabilities** – Financial obligations or debts owed by an individual or business.
- **Liquidity** – The ease with which an asset can be converted into cash.

M

- **Matching Transactions** – A Quicken feature that matches downloaded transactions with manually entered ones to prevent duplicates.
- **Mobile App** – The Quicken mobile application that allows users to manage their finances on the go.
- **Mortgage Tracker** – A tool in Quicken used to monitor mortgage payments and amortization.

N

- **Net Worth** – The total value of an individual's or business's assets minus liabilities.
- **Non-Discretionary Spending** – Essential expenses that cannot be easily reduced, such as rent and utilities.

O

- **Online Bill Pay** – A Quicken feature that allows users to pay bills directly from their bank accounts.
- **Overdraft Protection** – A banking service that prevents transactions from being declined due to insufficient funds.

P

- **Payee** – The recipient of a payment in a financial transaction.

- **Payroll Management** – A feature in Quicken Home & Business that helps track wages and employee payments.
- **Personal Finance Software** – Software designed to help individuals manage their money, such as Quicken.
- **Planned Transactions** – Transactions scheduled for future processing in Quicken.
- **Profit and Loss Report (P&L)** – A financial statement summarizing revenue, costs, and profits.

Q

- **Quicken Cloud** – A service that allows users to sync their financial data across multiple devices.
- **Quicken ID** – The unique login credential used to access Quicken services.

R

- **Reconciliation** – The process of ensuring Quicken records match bank and credit card statements.
- **Recurring Transaction** – An automated transaction that repeats on a set schedule.
- **Return on Investment (ROI)** – A measure of financial gain or loss from an investment relative to its cost.

S

- **Scheduled Payment** – A future-dated transaction set up in Quicken to pay bills automatically.
- **Security Code** – A unique number used for authentication in financial transactions.
- **Stock Ticker** – A symbol representing a publicly traded company in Quicken's investment tracking.

T

- **Tax Deduction** – An expense that reduces taxable income.
- **Tax Planning** – The process of organizing finances to minimize tax liabilities.
- **Third-Party Integration** – Connecting Quicken with other financial tools and services.

U

- **Uncategorized Transactions** – Transactions that do not have an assigned category.

V

- **Variable Expenses** – Costs that fluctuate from month to month, such as entertainment and dining out.

W

- **Wealth Management** – Strategies for growing and preserving financial assets.
- **Withholding** – The amount of income tax deducted from a paycheck.

Y

- **Year-End Summary** – A financial report that reviews income, expenses, and net worth over a full year.

Quicken Bible

Quicken Bible